La Bella Molisana

"Country Italian Cooking"

A culinary memoir of my family's favorite recipes

To order additional copies of this book, contact:
Xlibris
1-888-795-4274
www.Xlibris.com
Orders@Xlibris.com

A culinary memoir of my family's favorite recipes

La Bella Molisana
"Country Italian Cooking"

By

Marianna Iuliano Schiavone

PHOTOGRAPHS BY
Gerardo Iuliano

Dedication

    This book is dedicated to my beautiful family, for without them this book would not be possible. To Michelina and Donato, my mother and father, who taught me all about good food and the appreciation of fine things. Thank you to my Nonna Elvira for keeping the traditions alive. To my husband Tony, who supported me while I was working on this book and in whatever I choose to pursue. Also, to my brother Gerry, who always gives me a push to believe and follow my dreams, even when I think they are unattainable. And mostly, to my children, I hope that you grow to follow our family tradition of great food and wine and really enjoy the splendor of being Italian.

Special Thanks

I would like to take this time to recognize the women in my family for only because of them this book is possible. I am very fortunate to be blessed with a family that is so compassionate and admirable. With all of your assistance we now have a memento that we can pass on to our family and others.

Contents

Introduction

I remember waking up early on many Saturday mornings to the smell of fresh sauce in the air. Thinking I was in a dream until I came to my senses, I would find my mother in the kitchen frying meatballs for a huge pot of sauce. She would just look at me with a smile and say in Italian, " Hai sentuto l'odore" which meant "you couldn't resist the aroma". She was right. It was a great way to wake up in the morning. I love my mothers meatballs. Biting into one right after they were fried was the best way to eat them. They were warm, mouthwatering, moist and flavorful. An experience I will never forget. Because of my mother and the other women in my family I have many memories of food, cooking and the joys of sharing meals with those I love. Now that I have a family of my own I want to keep the aromas in the air, so they may enjoy food as I have.

My family originates from Molise, provincia d'Isernia, Italy. Most of them immigrated to North America at different times. They made their new homes in Canada, New York and Pennsylvania. Growing up then they had very little. They came to America in search of wealth and prosperity. Aside from making comfortable lives for themselves, my relatives passed down to their children the greatest gift of all, family togetherness and a great love of food and wine.

My family would rarely, except on special occasions, go to a restaurant for a meal. Restaurant meals always seemed to be missing something. Nothing ever tasted as good as what we made at home. There was nothing we didn't make either. At home we made pasta, cheese, sausage and wine. The list goes on and on. I think it is the passion for food and wine and the love for each other that makes it taste so good.

This book is a gathering of recipes from the women of my family. As the family grows, the traditions will slowly change, so this book will be a keepsake to remember all the great traditions our Italian family has grown to love. As our family grows apart and ends up in different locations, family gatherings will happen less and less. This is a very sad thought, so with this book of recipes we can hold on to a little bit of our heritage, from the most elegant meal to our everyday ones.

13

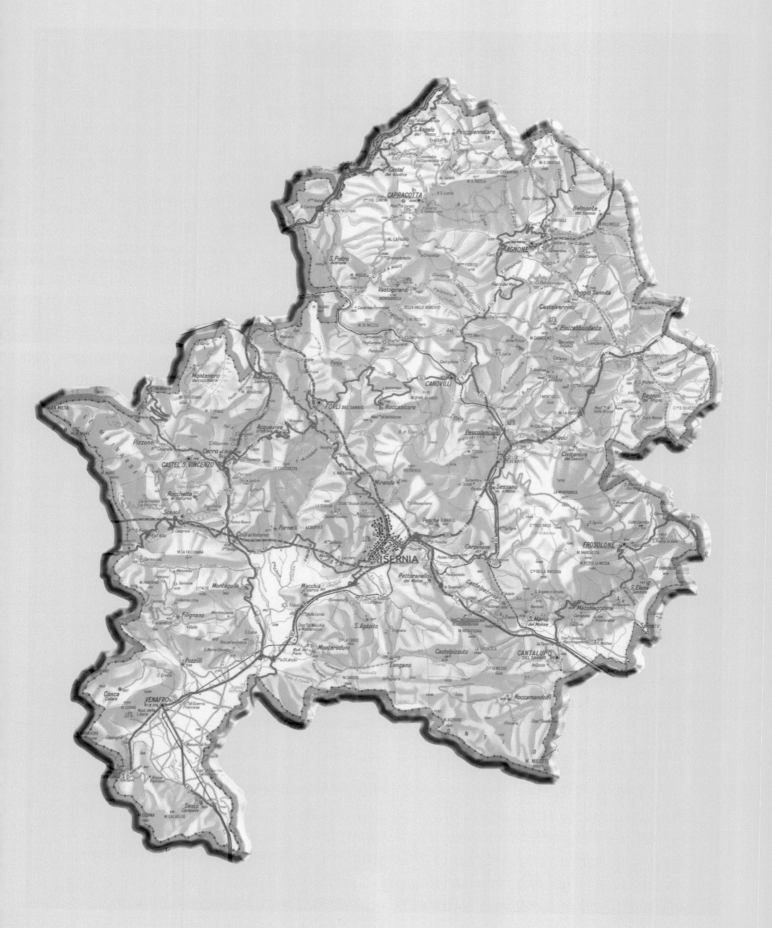

Molise

Molise is one of 20 regions that together make up Italy. Located east of Rome on the east coast of Italy, on the Adriatic Sea, its history can be traced back to prehistoric times. Scientists have discovered that some of the oldest inhabitants of Europe are from this area of the Apennines.

Molise-Abruzzi was once one region before it was divided in 1963 becoming two separate regions. Now, Molise finds itself to be one of the smallest regions of Italy, second only to Valle D'Aosta. Its total area is approximately 4438 sq. km (1714 sq. miles) with a population of about 330,000. Most of its people are spread out over the area in small villages. Campobasso and Isernia are the two provinces of Molise, as well as its major cities. Isernia became the region's capital in 1970. It is interesting to note that Isernia was actually the first capital of Italy around 100 BC.

The most prevalent industry in Molise is agriculture, which includes the cultivation of grain, fruits and vegetables. Wheat is the largest agriculture crop and is used in creating some of Italy's finest pasta. Other regional industries include wine making, food processing, furniture manufacturing and even the production of cement.

Because of varying climate and terrain throughout Italy, available fruit, vegetables and livestock differ from region to region. Each location prepares the same classic Italian dishes but with their own regional flair. From meat and pasta to wine and cheese, it is exciting to see, smell and taste Molise's own unique flavor in the Italian kitchen.

The people of Molise make all the Italian favorites: mozzarella di bufala, mushrooms, truffles, fish, bread, pizza, polenta, pasta, veal, pork sausage, salami, cappicola, sopressata, prosciutto, wine, olive oil, vinegar and tomato sauce they are all fresh, in season and fatto di casa (home made).

Molise offers a natural fresh beauty filled with tradition, emotion, color and passion for good food. It may be small but it is filled with ancient history, culture, folklore, beautiful landscapes and especially culinary delights. From within forests that have been around since ancient Roman times, you can discover wild mushrooms and even tartufi (truffles). Its rivers and mountain streams are still fresh and clear as are the beaches on the Adriatic coast. From these waters, fresh trout, pickled sting ray and frutta di mare are enjoyed. The high picturesque mountain ranges covered in trees make scenic walks seem timeless. A leisurely stroll may bring you past groves of fig and olive trees, centuries old, which cause you to wonder what life may have been like in ancient times.

Castelpetroso Santuario

Rising out of the hillside in the town of Castelpetroso in Molise is Il Santuario del'Addolorata. This cathedral built in the medieval style is to honor Maria Santissima Addolorata (the Virgin Mary), the patron saint of Molise. In 1888 a vision of Maria Santissima Addolorata was seen by two farm girls Fabiana Cicchino and Serafina Valentino. Two years later construction for the church began in 1890. It was promised that those who donated to the building of the cathedral would receive gratitude and blessings from Maria Santissima Addolorata herself. Due to destruction during the world wars and subsequent reconstruction, it was finally completed in 1975 funded entirely on donations. Every year on March 22nd a huge feast is dedicated to Maria Santissima Addolorata. People arrive by the bus loads to follow in a procession above the church on the hill were statues of the seven (dolori) sufferings of Mary are located.

Antipasti

Panini di Melanzane
(Eggplant Sandwich)

  1 eggplant (1 pound)
  2 eggs
  1 cup grated parmigiano cheese
1/2 teaspoon garlic powder
1/8 teaspoon black pepper
  1 teaspoon parsley
1/4 cup breadcrumbs (fine)
  3 tablespoons olive oil

Slice the eggplant into thin slices (about 1/4 inch thick)and set aside. In a bowl beat
the eggs then mix in the parmigiano cheese, garlic powder, black pepper, parsley and
breadcrumbs. Spread a thin layer of the breadcrumb mixture on one side of the sliced
eggplant. Place another slice of eggplant on top to form a sandwich. Clean off the side,
so that there are no breadcrumbs hanging over, and place in a pan with hot olive oil.
Cook one side then carefully turn it to the other side. When the eggplant is golden brown
remove it and let it drain on a paper towel. Slice the sandwiches into strips and serve.
Serve 6.

Bruschetta di Pomodori
(Toasted Bread with Tomatoes)

4 medium ripe tomatoes diced
1/2 teaspoon salt
1 clove of garlic (minced)
2 tablespoons water
2 tablespoons olive oil
6 leaves of basil chopped
1 tablespoon grated parmigiano cheese
    Italian bread sliced and toasted

Dice the tomatoes and put them in a bowl.
Next, add salt, garlic, water, olive oil, basil
and parmigiano cheese and mix together.
There should be a good amount of juice in
the bowl to cover the mixture. Place the
bowl in the refrigerator for a few hours.
Serves 6.

On the toasted Italian bread, spoon the
tomatoes on top with a little juice
and enjoy.

In my family we like to let our guests spoon
the tomatoes on themselves. The bread will
get soggy if the tomatoes sit on the bread
too long, so it is best to eat it right away.

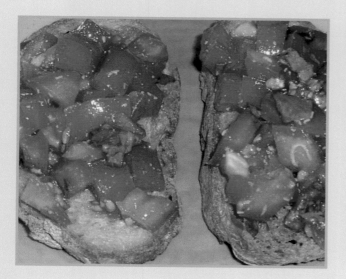

Crostini con Olive
(Olive Spread)

1 cup Calamata olives pitted
2 tablespoons olive oil
1/2 teaspoon garlic powder
1/2 teaspoon parsley
1/4 teaspoon black pepper
1/4 teaspoon sugar
1 teaspoon vinegar
1/2 cup shredded asiago cheese
    Italian bread sliced and toasted

Put all the ingredients together in a food
processor and blend until all you see are
little lumps of olive. Spoon on toasted
bread and sprinkle with asiago cheese.
Put them on a baking sheet and place in
the broiler until cheese is melted, about 3
minutes. Serves 6.

Buona sera buona notte, c'e un lupo
ha le porte, la porta casca giu, e lupo
non c'e piu. Ho girato la montagna,
e trovato 'na castagna la castagna
tutta mia, buona notte la compagnia.

Vongole Ripieni
(Stuffed Clams)

1 dozen clams
1/2 cup clam juice (water)
1/2 cup breadcrumbs
1 tablespoon olive oil
1/4 teaspoon garlic powder
1/4 teaspoon parsley
1/4 teaspoon salt
1/4 teaspoon black pepper
1/4 teaspoon oregano
1 medium tomato (finely chopped)

Steam the clams in a pot with shallow water. Once the clams have opened remove them from the water. Separate and clean shell halves. Strain the water with a cheesecloth or coffee filter and save, this is the clam juice. Remove the clam meat, rinse and finely chop it. In a bowl, mix the breadcrumbs, olive oil, garlic powder, parsley, salt, pepper, oregano, tomatoes, clam meat and clam juice. Fill the clam shells and broil for five minutes, until browned. Makes two dozen half shells. Serve cooled. Serves 6.

Taralli
(Italian Pretzels)

1 teaspoon yeast
1/4 cup sugar
4 cups all purpose flour
1/2 cup olive oil
1 tablespoon salt
2 teaspoons anise seeds
5 cups of water

Add the yeast and sugar in 1 cup of luke warm water. Let the yeast form a mushroom. On a work surface form a well with the flour and add the salt, anise seeds, olive oil and yeast mixture in the center. Slowly mix the center ingredients with the flour. Once the ingredients are all mixed work the dough until it is smooth. Cover the dough with a bowl and let it rest for 20 minutes. Next take little amounts of dough and roll it on the work surface with the palm off your hands until it forms a line (about the thickness of a pencil), then fold it into a circle or twist the ends (whatever shape you would like them to be). Place the shaped dough into a pot of boiling water. Once they begin to float remove them from the water and let them dry on a towel for about 5 minutes. Remove the heated oven racks from the oven and place the taralli right next to each other (no touching) on the racks and bake for a half hour or until golden brown at 350 degrees.
Makes 4 Dozen.

Olive Conditi
(Seasoned Olives)

2 cups black olives
1/2 teaspoon celery salt
1/2 teaspoon oregano
1/2 teaspoon garlic powder
1 tablespoon olive oil
1 teaspoon vinegar
1/4 teaspoon crushed peppers (optional)

Mix all the ingredients together. Serves 6.

Clockwise starting at the top left: Prosciutto e Melone;
Olive Conditti; Crostini con Olive; Vongole Ripieno.

Crostini con Ceci
(Toasted Bread with Garbanzo Paste)

1 15 ounce can garbanzo beans
5 tablespoons olive oil
1 teaspoon garlic powder
1/4 teaspoon salt
   Italian bread sliced and toasted

Drain the beans. In a food processor add all the ingredients and blend well. (If you are using fresh beans you will need to add more salt.) Serve at room temperature on toasted bread. Serves 6.

Extra virgin olive oil is a major ingredient in the Italian kitchen.

Prosciutto e Melone
(Prosciutto and Melon)

12 slices of honeydew melon
6 slices of prosciutto

Cut the prosciutto in half lengthwise. Wrap each slice of honeydew with a piece of prosciutto. Serves 6.

(Nonna Camilla Iuliano at her home in Cantalupo nel Sannio, Molise-Italia)

Quando la fame entra della porta,
l'amore esce della finestra

Nonna Camilla

Nonna Camilla Iuliano would visit America every few years. Everyone loved having her stay at their house. She is light hearted and funny not to mention a fantastic cook. She use to cook for her seven children and her husband in her tiny kitchen in Italy. Even though the kitchen was small, it served its purpose. She put out meals that shaped her children's memories. Country cooking at its best. All the seasonal favorites from pasta and minestra to salsiccia and patate. A small kitchen but a big heart.

Italian rhymes and Italian proverbs were Nonna Camilla's favorite things to recite to everyone. The ones in the Molisana dialect are the funniest. As children, we loved going on walks with her as she recited her poetry. She told us what Italy especially Cantalupo was like long ago. It was not until we were older that we would take her hand and walk down that country road in Cantalupo. Her stories seem to be more alive there. You could see, smell and even taste exactly what she meant. She loves her small town in Italy as much as we do. I guess that is why she never moved to America.

Zucchini con Aceto
(Zucchini with Vinegar)

1 medium zucchini
2 cups water
1 cup white vinegar
2 tablespoons sugar
1 tablespoon salt
4 basil leaves (chopped)
1 clove of garlic (minced)
2 tablespoons olive oil

Slice the zucchini thin, about 1/4 inch thick. In a pot mix the water, vinegar, sugar and salt. Bring to a boil. Add the zucchini and let it boil for 5 minutes, until tender. Strain the water and let the zucchini cool. Once cooled add the basil, garlic and olive oil. Refrigerate for 1 hour and serve. Serves 6.

Melanzane Marinata
(Marinated Eggplant)

1 large eggplant
1 tablespoon salt
2 cups water
2 tablespoons sugar
1 cup white vinegar
4 basil leaves (chopped)
1 clove of garlic (minced)
2 tablespoons olive oil

Peel the eggplant and slice it about 1/4 inch thick. In a large bowl make layers with the eggplant. Salt every layer very well. Put a paper towel on top and place a weight on top of it to squeeze the eggplant. (For this step you can use a marble slab if you have one or whatever you have that weighs about 5 pounds.) Let this sit for 24 hours. After 24 hours rinse the eggplant well and squeeze them individually to remove the water. In a pot, add the water, sugar and vinegar and bring to a boil. Add the eggplant and let it boil for 2 minutes. Strain the water and lay out the eggplant on a plate to cool. Once cooled, add the basil, garlic and olive oil. Refrigerate for 1 hour and serve. Serves 6.

Puponelle Ripieni
(Stuffed Cherry Peppers)

12 cherry peppers (pickled)
 4 slices of prosciutto (or 12 anchovies)
12 cubes of provolone cheese

Core out the cherry peppers. Cut the prosciutto into slices so they fit around the cheese cubes. Wrap the provolone cubes with a piece of prosciutto and stuff it in the center of the cherry peppers. Serves 4.

Fiori di Zucchini Ripieni
(Stuffed Zucchini Flowers)

4 ounces asiago cheese
2 dozen zucchini flowers
1 cup flour
1 cup milk
1/4 cup grated parmigiano cheese
1/2 teaspoon salt
1/2 cup olive oil

Cut the asiago into thick strips. Place a slice into each flower and set aside. In a bowl mix the flour, milk, parmigiano cheese and salt together to form a batter. Heat the olive oil in a frying pan, then dip each flower in the batter and place them in the pan. Fry until batter is golden brown. Remove them from the pan and lay them out on paper towels to drain off excess oil. Serves 6.

Un Piatto di Salumi e Formaggi
(Meat and Cheese Platter)

1/2 pound provolone cheese (sliced)
 1 pound parmigiano cheese (chunks)
1/2 pound prosciutto slices
1/2 pound salami (sliced)
1/2 pound dry sausage (sliced)

Arrange meats and cheeses on a platter in your own style. (If you do not have or like these meat and cheeses substitute them with other Italian items.)

This is the most popular appetizer in Italian households. Everybody loves to eat these meats and cheeses and it is very easy to make. In my family most of these items are homemade. Serves 6.

Peperoni Arrostiti
(Roasted Peppers)

4 red bell peppers
1/2 teaspoon salt
1/2 teaspoon garlic powder
 1 tablespoon olive oil

Blacken the peppers all around on a grill or under the broiler. Once they are blackened place them in a paper bag and close it for 5 minutes. Remove the peppers from the bag and peel off the skin. Then, take out the core and seeds and cut the pepper into slices. Place the peeled pepper slices in a bowl and add the salt, garlic powder and olive oil. Mix well and enjoy. Serves 6.

Carpinone

On a peak, in the beautiful town of Carpinone, stands Castel Caldora. This castle was built for Antonio Caldora in the 13th century AD after the devastating earthquake in 1456. After many years, it was permanently dedicated to Alfonso d'Aragona who remained there in hospitality of Antonio Caldera. In 1064 a monastery and church were built on that same peak and the town was then built around it. Below the town flows the Carpino river and so comes the name for the town Carpinone. The population of Carpinone today is about 1,200 people.

Macchiagodena

In 964 AD, when Macchiagodena was established until 1815, the town was owned by many different families. The last family to own Macchiagodena to date was Nicola Centomani. Don Nicola owned a lot of the surrounding land. My mothers family lived in Santa Maria del Molise the town just below Macchiagodena. Her family planted and harvested wheat on land owned by descendants of Don Nicola. After the harvest, they would have to pay the amount of a huge sack of grain to La Signora Don Nicola.

Verdure

Patate Schiacciate
(Italian Mashed Potatoes)

8 medium potatoes
2 tablespoons salt
1/3 cup olive oil
1 teaspoon garlic powder
1 teaspoon oregano

Peel and cut up the potatoes. In a pot of water add the potatoes and salt. Cook over medium heat until thoroughly cooked. When potatoes are done strain them and put them in a bowl. Mash them with a fork. Add enough olive oil to gloss the potatoes. Next add the garlic and oregano. If more salt is needed add to taste. Serves 4.

Broccoli di Rapini Fritti
(Fried Rapini)

2 tablespoons olive oil
1 clove of garlic (minced)
1 bunch of mustard greens
1/4 teaspoon salt
4 eggs
1/4 cup milk
2 tablespoons parmigiano cheese

In a frying pan heat the olive oil and fry the garlic until golden. Add the mustard greens and salt. Fry the greens until they are cooked down and let simmer. In a bowl beat eggs, milk and parmigiano cheese. Add the egg mixture to the mustard greens and simmer until eggs are cooked. Serves 4.

Pizza di Patate
(Potato Pizza)

9   potatoes
6   eggs
1   cup salami cubed
1   cup dry sausage cubed
1   cup mozzarella cheese grated
8   hard boiled eggs chopped
2   teaspoons salt
1/2 teaspoon black pepper
1   teaspoon garlic powder
1   tablespoon parsley

Place the potatoes in boiling water until fully cooked. Then press them though a potato ricer. Beat the eggs into the potatoes. Next mix in the salami, sausage, mozzarella cheese, hard boiled eggs, salt, pepper, garlic and parsley. Press mixture in a well greased baking pan and cover with foil. Cook until golden brown about 45 minutes at 375 degrees. Serves 6.

Insalata di Patate
(Italian Potato Salad)

6   potatoes
1   tablespoon salt
1/4 cup olive oil
2   tablespoons oregano
1   tablespoon garlic powder

Peel and cut potatoes in big cubes. In a pot of water add the potatoes and salt. Cook until tender. Once they are cooked strain the water and transfer the potatoes to a bowl. Add 2 tablespoons of olive oil, let them cool. When they have cooled add the remaining olive oil, oregano, and garlic powder. Refrigerate and serve cold. Serves 6.

Frittata di Bietola
(Swiss Chard Omelet)

1   bunch of Swiss chard
2   tablespoons butter
6   eggs
1/2 cup milk
3   tablespoons parmigiano cheese
1   teaspoon garlic powder or 1 clove of garlic (minced)
1/2 teaspoon salt
1/2 teaspoon black pepper

Wash and chop the Swiss chard. In a frying pan, over medium heat melt the butter and add the Swiss chard. Cover the pan and stir occasionally until the greens have cooked down. In a bowl beat the eggs and milk. Next, add the parmigiano cheese, garlic powder, salt and black pepper, stir well. Pour the egg mixture into the pan with the greens, cover and cook over medium heat. When one side is cooked turn it over and cook the other side*. Continue cooking uncovered until golden. Serves 6.

*To turn over the frittata, slide it out of the pan onto a plate, place the pan over the top of the plate and with hot pads on grab the pan and plate and flip the uncooked side onto the pan.

Fave Fritte
(Fried Fava Beans)

1/2 large onion sliced
4   tablespoons olive oil
3   cups fava beans (fresh)
1/2 teaspoon salt
2   cups water
    dash black pepper

In a frying pan on medium heat, sauté the sliced onion in olive oil until golden. Add the fava beans, salt, pepper and water. Cover and let it cook for 15 minutes, stirring occasionally to avoid sticking. Remove the cover and continue to cook until the water has evaporated and the fava beans are tender. Serves 6.

Frittata di Zucchini
(Zucchini Omelet)

1 medium zucchini
3 tablespoons olive oil
6 eggs
1/2 cup milk
3 tablespoons parmigiano cheese
1 teaspoon garlic powder
1/2 teaspoon salt
1/2 teaspoon black pepper

Wash the zucchini and slice it thin. In a frying pan, over medium heat add the olive oil and zucchini. Cover the pan and stir occasionally until the zucchini has softened. In a bowl beat the eggs and milk, add the parmigiano cheese, garlic powder, salt and black pepper, stir well. Pour the egg mixture into the pan with the zucchini, cover and cook over medium heat. When one side is cooked turn it over and cook the other side*. Continue cooking uncovered until golden.
Serves 6.

*To turn over the frittata, slide it out of the pan onto a plate, place the pan over the top of the plate and with hot pads on grab the pan and plate and flip the uncooked side onto the pan.

La frittata é fatta!-
(The damage is done!)

Funghi Ripieni
(Stuffed Mushrooms)

1 dozen Crimini mushrooms
4 tablespoons olive oil
1/2 cup breadcrumbs
1 teaspoon garlic powder
2 tablespoons parmigiano cheese
1 egg

Wash the mushrooms and cut off the stems. Set the caps aside. Chop the stems into little pieces and sauté them in 2 tablespoons of olive oil. Remove the stems from the pan and place in a bowl. Mix in the breadcrumbs, cheese, garlic powder and egg. Stuff this filling into the mushroom caps. In a baking dish drizzle some olive oil on the bottom and add the mushrooms. Drizzle olive oil on the top of the mushrooms. Bake for 20 minutes at 350 degrees. Serves 4.

Zucchini Ripieni
(Stuffed Zucchini)

3 small zucchini
1/4 cup breadcrumbs
3 tablespoons olive oil
1/4 teaspoon salt
1 egg
3 tablespoons parmigiano cheese
1/4 teaspoon garlic powder

Cut the zucchini in half lengthwise.
Spoon out the center and save it. In a bowl
mix the zucchini center, breadcrumbs, 2
tablespoons of olive oil, salt, garlic powder,
egg and parmigiano cheese. Mix well and
fill the cored zucchini with the mixture.
Place the zucchini in a baking pan, drizzle
the remaining olive oil on top and sprinkle
with parmigiano cheese. Bake for 25
minutes at 375 degrees. Serves 6.

Insalata di Fagiolini
(String Bean Salad)

2 pounds fresh string beans
4 quarts of water
11/2 tablespoons salt
1/4 cup peeled julienne almonds
1 teaspoon garlic powder
1 medium diced tomato
1 tablespoon olive oil
2-3 tablespoons balsamic vinegar
      salt to taste

Wash and snap the ends of the beans
off. Cut them in half. In a 5 quart pot
bring the water to a boil and add 11/2
tablespoons of salt and the beans. Cook
them until they are tender but crisp.
Strain the beans then flush them with
cold water. In a bowl add the beans,
almonds, garlic powder and tomato.
Add a few dashes of salt, olive oil and
vinegar and stir. Refrigerate and serve
them chilled. Serves 8.

Tutto il giorno minestra e patate.
E quando viene la festa
patate e minestra

Piselli con Funghi
(Peas with Mushrooms)

1/4 large onion sliced
1   4 ounce can of sliced mushrooms
    (or 1/2 cup fresh sliced mushrooms)
1   pound frozen petite peas
1/4 teaspoon salt

In a frying pan heat the olive oil on
medium heat, sauté the sliced onion
and mushrooms until golden. (If using
fresh mushrooms, slice and boil prior
to sautéing.) Add the peas and salt
and continue frying uncovered. Stir
about 10 minutes, until the peas
become tender. Serves 6.

Peperoni Fritti
(Fried Peppers)

1   dozen banana peppers (hot or mild)
1/2 cup olive oil
    dash of salt

Wash and dry the peppers. Cut off the
tops of the peppers and slice them in
half lengthwise. In a frying pan
pre-heat the oil. Next, add the peppers
and brown them on both sides.
Remove them from the pan and salt.
Enjoy them on a slice of plain bread or
in a panino (sandwich).

Fiori di Zucchini Impanati Fritti
(Battered Fried Zucchini Flowers)

1   cup flour
1   cup milk
1/4 cup grated parmigiano cheese
1/2 teaspoon salt
2   dozen zucchini flowers

Mix the flour, milk, parmigiano cheese and salt together to form a batter. In a frying pan heat the olive oil. Dip each flower in the batter then place them in the pan. Fry until batter is golden brown. Remove them from the pan and lay them out on paper towels to drain off excess oil. Serves 6.

Zucchini al Forno
(Baked Zucchini)

1   cup pancake mix
4   eggs
3   cups diced zucchini
1/2 cup chopped onions
2   tablespoons chopped parsley
1/2 cup romano cheese
1/2 cup olive oil
1/4 teaspoon garlic powder
1/2 teaspoon salt
1/2 teaspoon oregano

In a large bowl beat the pancake mix and eggs together. Next add the zucchini, onions, parsley, romano cheese, olive oil, garlic powder, salt and oregano and mix well. Pour the mixture into a well greased baking pan (9x13). Bake for 45 minutes at 350 degrees. Serves 6.

In the region of Molise you can go from the beautiful ski resort of Campitello Matese to the white sand beaches of Termoli in about a hour by car.

Bojano

The busy little town of Boiano (Bojano) has its fair share of people in its streets. Whether they are shopping in a salumeria, gelateria or mercato, these Molisani like to be moving around. The sound of church bells are loud and exciting during any given feast. This town is home to one of the oldest churches in the area. La Chiesa Rupestra di Sant'Egidio was completed in 850 AD. Most of the church was destroyed over its life through disasters and wars, but it has been restored recently with its original abbey.

I Primi

Risotto alla Milanese
(Milanese Rice)

1/2 cup butter
1 medium onion (chopped)
4 cups chicken stock
2 cups rice
6 mushrooms (chopped)
2 strands of saffron

In a large pan over medium heat melt the butter and sauté the onion. Meanwhile, in a separate pot boil the chicken stock. Pour the rice into the melted butter and onions and stir until golden brown. Add the mushrooms and saffron. Then, pour the stock in one ladle at a time, stirring the rice as it absorbs the stock and becomes fluffy. Serves 6.

Pasta Primavera
(Springtime Pasta)

4 tablespoons olive oil
3 chicken breasts (cubed)
1 cup peas
1 medium onion (finely chopped)
1 green pepper (chopped)
3 mushrooms (sliced)
1 carrot (chopped)
1 tomato (chopped)
1 teaspoon salt
1/4 teaspoon black pepper
1 pound penne pasta

In a large pan heat the olive oil, then add the chicken, vegetables, salt and pepper. Cook over medium heat until tender. Meanwhile, cook the penne pasta, then strain it. Return the pasta to the pot and add the chicken and vegetables and cook together for about 1 minute. Serves 4.

Piove e ce' il sole
La Madonna coglie un fiore
lo coglio per Gesù
e domani non piove piu

Zuppa degli Sposi
(Wedding Soup)

Broth
5 quarts of water
1 whole chicken
1 tablespoon salt
1 cup carrots
4 stalks of celery
1 large onion
1 large tomato chopped
1 teaspoon parsley (chopped)
  pinch of baking soda

Meatballs
1/2 pound ground pork
1/4 pound ground veal or beef
 1 tablespoon parmigiano cheese
1/4 teaspoon salt
1/4 teaspoon black pepper
1/2 teaspoon garlic powder
 1 teaspoon parsley (chopped)
 3 eggs
1/2 cup breadcrumbs
  olive oil

Omelet
 6 large eggs
1/4 teaspoon salt
  dash of pepper
 1 tablespoon parmigiano cheese
 2 tablespoons olive oil

Broth
In a large pot bring 5 quarts of water to a boil. Cut the chicken into pieces. Add the salt and chicken to the boiling water. Reduce the heat and skim off the foam as it accumulates and let the chicken cook for about a half hour. As the chicken cooks, begin with the omelet and meatballs (see below).

After a half hour add the carrots, celery, onion, tomato, parsley and a pinch of baking soda to the pot. Continue cooking until the chicken is fully cooked about another half hour. Remove the chicken breasts when they are fully cooked, cut them up into little cubes and set aside. Add 4 cups of water and continue cooking until the vegetables are tender. When the vegetables are done remove them and the remaining chicken from the broth. Chop up the vegetables and set aside. Strain the broth so it is clear and return it to the pot.

Add 8 more cups of water and bring it back to a boil. Once the stock has reached a boil add the meatballs and chopped chicken. Lower the heat to a simmer and continue to cook for 15 more minutes. Next add the vegetables and omelet squares to the soup and simmer for an additional half hour.

Omelet
Beat all the ingredients together. On a low heat in a frying pan heat up the olive oil then add enough egg mixture to cover the bottom of the pan. Cook one side then flip it to cook the other side. Once golden brown remove the omelet from the pan and let it drain on a paper towel. Continue this process with the remainder of the eggs. Allow the omelets to cool, then cut them into little squares and set aside.

Meatballs
In a large bowl add the pork, veal, parmigiano cheese, salt, pepper, garlic powder, parsley and eggs. Mix well, then add the breadcrumbs. In a frying pan cover the bottom with olive oil and heat on medium. Form the meatballs and place them in the frying pan. Fill the pan with the meatballs, one next to the other with very little room between them. Turn the meatballs when they are golden on the bottom and cook the opposite side just the same. Serves 8.

Di venerdi e di marte
no si sposa e non si parte

Lasagna al Forno
(Baked Lasagna)

2 tablespoons salt
1 pound lasagna noodles
2 pounds ricotta cheese
1 teaspoon salt
5 eggs
2 teaspoons garlic powder
4 tablespoons parmigiano cheese
5 cups tomato sauce (Salsa di Pomodoro recipe-doubled)
10 meatballs sliced (Polpette recipe)
2 cups mozzarella cheese (grated)

In a large pot of boiling water add 2 tablespoons of salt and lasagna noodles.
Cook until the noodles are al dente. Meanwhile, in a bowl mix the ricotta cheese,
1 teaspoon of salt, eggs, garlic powder and parmigiano cheese and set aside. When
the noodles are done remove the pot from the heat and pour most of the water out
and add some cold water, this will stop the cooking process and you will be able
to handle the pasta. In a deep baking pan, add some tomato sauce to cover the
bottom then make one layer of the noodles so the edges are overlapping. Next put
some more sauce on the noodles and spread with half of the ricotta mixture, add a
layer of sliced meatballs and top with mozzarella cheese. Do the layers over once
more and top it with a row of noodles then sauce. Cover the pan with foil and
bake for 45 minutes. Serves 10.

Taconelle e Fagioli
(Homemade Pasta with Beans)

Taconelle
    4   cups flour
    1/2 cup semolina flour
    3   eggs
    l 1/2 cup water

Fagioli
    2   cups beans (your choice)
    1/2 teaspoon salt
    4   tomatoes (chopped)
    1/2 cup fresh basil (chopped)
    1   teaspoon garlic powder
    1/2 teaspoon celery salt
    2   tablespoons olive oil

Taconelle
Mix the flour and semolina flour together and make a hole in the middle. Break the eggs into the middle and beat, add the water to the eggs. Begin working the flour into the eggs, add more water if needed. Once all the flour is incorporated into the eggs begin kneading the dough until it becomes relaxed and easy to work. Form a ball with the dough and place it in a oiled bowl and cover it with plastic wrap. Let the dough rest for 1-1/2 hours. Next roll out the dough into a round circle about 1/8" thick. Then fold the dough in half and then in half again. Cut strips of the pasta lengthwise about 1" thick then cut out 1" pieces along those strips to form little squares. Lay the pasta squares on a baking sheet and put them in the freezer until you are ready to use them.

Fagioli
In a pot add the beans, salt and enough water to cover the beans. Cook until the beans are almost done then drain the water and transfer the beans to a bowl and set aside. (Remove the film on top of the water while the beans cook.) In a large sauce pan heat the olive oil then add the tomatoes, basil, garlic powder and celery salt. Bring the sauce to a boil reduce to medium heat and add the beans. Continue cooking until the beans are fully cooked.

Next, cook the pasta and strain most of the water, leaving about 1 cup of water in the pan. Add the bean mixture to the pot and stir. Serves 6.

Taconelle are normally cut into squares.

Pasta con Zucca di Burro
(Pasta with Butternut Squash)

1 medium butternut squash
3/4 cup olive oil
1/2 teaspoon salt
1/2 teaspoon garlic powder
1/4 teaspoon black pepper
1 teaspoon parsley
1/2 cup pine nuts
1 pound pasta
1/4 cup parmigiano cheese

Cut the butternut squash in half and clean out the seeds. Next, cut it into quarters. Place the squash on a baking sheet and bake it for 1 hour at 350 degrees or place in a microwave safe bowl and add a cup of water and cook for 20 minutes. When the squash is soft and tender it is ready. Drain the water and allow it to cool so you can handle the pieces. Peel off the skin with a knife and dice up the squash. In a large frying pan heat the olive oil and add the diced squash. Season with salt, garlic, pepper and parsley. Stir and cook for 10 minutes over medium heat. Next, add the pine nuts and continue cooking for 5 minutes then lower the heat to a simmer. While the squash is simmering cook the pasta. Right before you strain the pasta add the parmigiano cheese to the squash and stir, remove it from the heat. Drain the pasta and add the squash to it. Sprinkle with shredded parmigiano cheese. Serves 6.

Pasta con Tartufi
(Pasta with Truffles)

1 pound penne pasta
1 tablespoon salt
1/4 teaspoon salt
1 pint heavy cream
1 teaspoon tartufi (jarred or fresh)
2 tablespoons parmigiano cheese

In a medium sauce pan heat the heavy cream, 1/4 teaspoon salt, and parmigiano cheese. Bring to a quick boil then turn off the heat, stirring to prevent sticking. In a 5 quart pot boil enough water to cook the pasta freely, then add 1 tablespoon salt and the pasta, cook until the pasta is al dente. Drain the water and return the pasta to the pot. Next add the cream mixture to the pasta and cook on high heat. Keep stirring until the cream begins to coat the pasta. Remove from the heat then stir in the tartufi. Serves 4.

Salsa di Pomodoro
(Quick Sauce for Pasta)

  2 tablespoons olive oil
1/2 cup chopped onion
  2 15 ounce cans stewed tomatoes
1/2 teaspoon salt
1/2 teaspoon garlic powder or 1 clove of garlic
      (minced)
  2 tablespoons dried basil or 5 fresh leaves
      (chopped)
      pinch of baking soda
      pinch of sugar

In a medium sauce pan heat the olive oil
then sauté the onions. Next, add the
tomatoes, salt, garlic and basil. Boil for 5
minutes, stirring occasionally, then add the
baking soda and sugar. Turn the heat down
and let the sauce simmer for 20 minutes.
Add to a pound of your favorite pasta and
enjoy. Serves 6.

Tagliatelle Con Brodo
(Pasta with Broth)

Pasta
  4 cups flour
1/2 cup semolina flour
  3 eggs
1/2 cup water

Broth
  6 cups water
  1 pound of chicken or beef
1/2 teaspoon salt
  1 teaspoon garlic powder
1/2 teaspoon celery salt
  4 tomatoes

Pasta
Mix the flour and semolina flour together
and make a hole in the middle. Break the
eggs into the middle and beat, add the
water to the eggs. Begin working the flour
into the eggs, add more water if needed.
Once all the flour is incorporated into the
eggs begin kneading the dough until it
becomes easier and well blended. Form a
ball with the dough and place it in a oiled
bowl and cover it with plastic wrap. Let
the dough rest for 1-1/2 hours. Next roll
out the dough into a round circle about
1/8" thick. Then fold the dough in half and
then in half again. Cut long strips of the
pasta 1/4" thick then cut those pieces about
6" in length. Place the pasta strips on a
baking sheet and put them in the freezer
until you are ready to use them.

Broth
In a large pot add the water, chicken or
beef, salt, garlic powder and celery salt.
Bring the water to a boil and cook for 10
minutes. Reduce the heat to a simmer and
add the tomatoes. Continue to cook for
20 minutes.

Next, cook the pasta separately and strain
the water. Add the pasta to the pot of broth
and stir. Serves 6.

Lasagna Rolotini
(Lasagna Rolls)

1 pound lasagna noodles
2 pounds ricotta cheese
1 teaspoon salt
1 teaspoon garlic powder
2 tablespoons parmigiano cheese
4 eggs
1 cup chopped spinach
1 cup mozzarella cheese (grated)
5 cups tomato sauce (Salsa di Pomodoro recipe-doubled)

In a large pot of water, cook the lasagna noodles. When the noodles are cooked, drain most of the water and add cold water in the pot. In a large bowl, mix the ricotta, salt, garlic powder, parmigiano cheese and eggs. Next, add the spinach and mozzarella cheese to the ricotta mixture.

To make the rolls, first, line the bottom of the pan with 1/2 cup tomato sauce. Stack two pieces of paper towel on each other and lay out some of the lasagna noodles, pat them dry with another piece of paper towel. Add 2 tablespoons of filling down the center of each noodle then roll it. Place the rolls in the pan next to each other. When you have completed rolling and lining the pan with all the noodles cover them with the remaining tomato sauce. Cover the pan with foil and bake for 45 minutes at 375 degrees. Serves 6.

Tortellini Cremosi
(Creamy Tortellini)

1 15 ounce can crushed tomatoes
1/2 cup chopped basil
1/4 teaspoon salt
1/2 teaspoon garlic powder
    pinch of baking soda
 1 cup heavy cream
1/2 cup parmigiano or asiago cheese
 2 tablespoons salt
 1 pound tortellini

In a medium sauce pan add the crushed tomatoes, basil, salt and garlic powder. Bring to a boil and add a pinch of baking soda and stir. Reduce the heat to a simmer and add the heavy cream and cheese. Meanwhile, in a pot of boiling water add 2 tablespoons of salt and the tortellini. Cook until the pasta is "al dente" then strain out the water. Return the tortellini to the pot and add the sauce. Continue cooking over medium heat stirring until the sauce begins to thicken on the pasta, about 2 minutes. Remove from the heat and serve. Serves 4

Finché c'è vita c'è speranza

Crespelle con Spinache e Ricotta
(Spinach and Ricotta Crêpes)

Crêpes
1 1/4 cup warm milk
1 cup flour
3 eggs
1/8 teaspoon salt
1 teaspoon oil

Filling
1 bunch spinach (chopped)
2 tablespoons butter
2 pounds ricotta cheese
4 tablespoons parmigiano cheese
5 eggs

Sauce
1 cup tomato sauce (Salsa di Pomodoro recipe)
1 pint heavy cream

Crêpes
In a bowl mix the warm milk and flour together. Beat the eggs and add it to the mixture along with the salt and oil. Mix well. Over a low heat in a small omelet non-stick pan, pour 2 tablespoons of the mixture in the pan moving it around until it does not go any further. Once the bottom has cooked turn it over with a fork and cook the other side. Makes 18 crêpes.

Sauce
In a medium pan combine the tomato sauce and heavy cream. Simmer just until heated.

Filling
Cook and drain the spinach. Squeeze out the water and chop. In a pan melt the butter, then add the spinach and cook until the butter is absorbed. In a bowl, mix the ricotta, parmigiano cheese, eggs, and spinach.

To stuff the crêpes add about 2 tablespoons of filling and roll the crêpe. Line a baking pan with 1/2 cup sauce and place the rolls next to each other. Once all the crêpes are lined in the pan pour the remaining sauce over the top of the crêpes. Cover the pan with foil and bake at 350° for 45 minutes. Serves 6.

San Massimo

Walking into a small and sparsely populated town like San Massimo takes you back to medieval times when pragmatic crafts, potions, malocchio (evil eye) and obscure cures for illnesses were all part of everyday life. Quaint little towns and villages like this one which speckle the hillside still continue in traditions that are now a cross between beliefs of both Pagan and Christian origin. Celebrations that were once centered around the earth, seasons and Roman gods are now Christian religious holidays and feasts.

Campomarino

The smell of anise fills the spring air as you pass fennel fields on old country roads in Campomarino. Located just south of Termoli, this seaside town is home to some of Molise's best wineries and olive oil companies.

Nonna Elvira

Born in the town of Cantalupo del Sannio, Elvira Pizzi has lived through two world wars. Her story of famine and hardship seem so unbelievable to people today. Her family, as well as most from that time, had little or nothing to eat. Her children would follow people eating oranges and wait for peels to fall to the ground which they would pick up and eat them as if they were candy. It is sad but true. Nonna Elvira would scrounge up anything that was eatable and manage to put together a meal that the whole family appreciated. Whether it was dry lintels, greens from the roadside or just potato skins with pork fat, it was a meal.

After the wars meals seem to be easier to put together. A 14 km walk to the next town of Boiano, Nonna would buy salt, shoes, baskets, cloth and other items they could afford. Fresh vegetables were grown in their garden, animals were raised on their property and wheat and corn were grown on leased land. She tells about how they had wheat ground into flour to make pasta and bread. She claims that it still tastes better than wheat flour we buy nowadays.

Nonna Elvira immigrated to the United States of America in February 1956, on the Andrea Doria three months before its historic sinking. She now lives in Northern California and is happy to make all the traditional meals as she did when she was living in Italy. Her bread and pizza are delicious and unforgettable. Home made pasta that she still cuts by hand and sauce made from tomatoes fresh from the garden are her favorites. Everyone loves Nonna Elvira's food, but they love her even more.

Nonna Elvira's Bread

4 1/2 cups water
  1 envelope yeast
  2 teaspoons sugar
  5 pounds bread flour
  2 tablespoons salt
  2 tablespoons margarine or butter
1/3 cup olive oil

Warm 2 cups of water to luke warm, then, add the yeast and sugar. Stir and let it sit until it foams into a mushroom. In a large bowl, mix the flour and salt together. Melt the margarine with 1/2 cup of hot water. Add the yeast mixture to the flour and mix. Pour the melted margarine or butter in the mix and continue working the dough. Add more water as it absorbs (1/2 cup at a time). Continue working the dough by punching it. Scrape the sides of the bowl with your fingers to gather all the dough and flour. Once all gathered add the oil and continue punching until the oil is well blended and the dough is smooth. Smooth the top and cover with wax paper, a dish towel and then a folded table cloth. Set aside and let it rise until the dough becomes twice its size. (About 2 hours) Once the dough has risen punch it down and let it rise again. (This time it will rise faster, about 1/2 hour). Transfer the dough to your work surface and cut the bread to the pan size you want and shape the dough, trying not to handle it too much. Cover the pans with dish towels and let the dough rise again. Bake at 400 degrees for 50 minutes until golden.

* You can add rosemary or olives to the dough to make it a specialty bread.

** This bread recipe is also what my family uses as pizza dough. Just stretch the dough out to fit your pan and brush with olive oil and top with your favorite toppings.

I Secondi

Salsiccia con Peperoni e Patate
(Sausage with Peppers and Potatoes)

6 tablespoons olive oil
6 Italian sausage (hot or mild)
8 potatoes sliced
1 teaspoon garlic powder or 1 clove of garlic
   (minced)
2 teaspoons salt
1 red bell peppers diced
1 green bell peppers diced
1 small onion diced

In a pan over medium heat, add 2 tablespoons of olive oil and brown the sausage. Once browned remove sausage and slice. Set aside. In the same pan add 4 tablespoons of olive oil to cover the bottom, then add the potatoes, garlic and salt. Cook over medium heat and stir occasionally (if potatoes start to become too dry add a couple more tablespoons of olive oil). When the potatoes are about half way done add the peppers and onion. Stir occasionally. When peppers become halfway done add the sausage back into the pan and cook until peppers are tender. (Add more salt if necessary). Serves 6.

Scaloppini di Vittello
(Veal Scaloppini)

2 eggs
1 cup breadcrumbs
3 tablespoons parmigiano cheese
1 pound veal (thinly sliced)
4 tablespoons olive oil

In a bowl, beat the eggs and set aside. In a flat plate, mix the breadcrumbs and parmigiano cheese and spread it flat. Dip the veal piece by piece into the eggs. Then dip them into the breadcrumbs covering both sides. Fry the meat in a pan with hot olive oil until golden brown on both sides (Add more olive oil as you need it). Serves 4.

Il vino è il latte dei vecchi

Arrosto Maiale
(Pork Roast)

1   tablespoon salt
1   tablespoon garlic powder
1   tablespoon black pepper
1/2 cup fresh parsley (chopped)
5-7 pound pork shoulder

In a small bowl combine the seasonings. Place the roast on a cutting board and poke deep holes into it with a sharp knife. Make a lot of holes. After each incision add a pinch of seasoning and push it in each hole as far as possible. Continue to poke and season on all sides of the roast, approximately 2 inches apart. Rub the remaining seasonings all over the roast. Place the meat into a roasting pan and cover. Bake for 2 hours or more at 450 degrees, until the meat is fully cooked and moist. Serves 6 to 8.

Braciole
(Meat Rolls)

4   pounds round steak (cut-thin about 1/4")
1   cup parsley (chopped)
2   teaspoons salt
1   teaspoon pepper
1 1/2 teaspoons garlic powder
    string to tie the meat
1/2 cup parmigiano cheese
1   cup olive oil
3/4 cup red wine
1/2 cup water
    tomato sauce

Lay the meat out flat and season with salt, pepper, parsley, garlic and parmigiano cheese. Roll the meat up and tie it with string. In a pot with hot olive oil, brown the meat rolls on both sides. When they are all browned add the wine and water to the pot and let the meat simmer for about 25 minutes. When they are done cooking add them to the tomato sauce and let it simmer for about 1 to 2 hours. To serve, remove the string and slice or you can leave them whole. Serves 12.

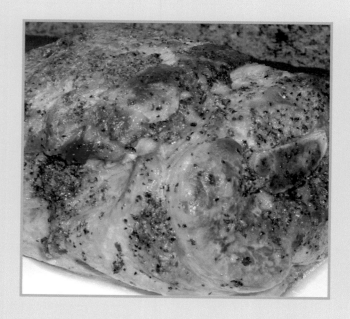

Polpette di Pasqua
(Easter Meatballs)

2 pounds ground pork
1 pound ground veal or beef
1 teaspoon salt
1 teaspoon black pepper
2 teaspoons garlic powder
4 tablespoons parmigiano cheese
4 teaspoons parsley
6 eggs
12 hard boiled eggs
2 cups breadcrumbs
1 cup olive oil

In a large bowl mix the pork, veal, salt, black pepper, garlic powder, parmigiano cheese, parsley and eggs. Next, add the breadcrumbs and mix well. In a frying pan cover the bottom with olive oil and heat on medium. Form the meatballs around the hard-boiled eggs and place them in the frying pan one next to the other with very little room between them. Turn the meatballs when they are golden on the bottom and cook the opposite side just the same. (Remove them from the pan and add them to a pot of sauce). Serves 12.

Pollo Impanato Fritto
(Breaded Chicken Strips)

24 boneless chicken strips
1/2 teaspoon salt
2 eggs
1/4 cup milk
1 1/2 cups breadcrumbs
3 tablespoons parmigiano cheese
1 teaspoon garlic powder
1/2 cup olive oil

Clean and salt the chicken. In a small bowl beat the eggs and milk. In a medium bowl mix the breadcrumbs, parmigiano cheese and garlic powder. Add olive oil to a frying pan on medium heat, just enough to cover the bottom (add more as needed). Dip the chicken in the egg mixture, then in the breadcrumbs and place them in the heated oil. Cook the chicken until golden brown, turning once. Serves 6.

Pollo e Patate al Forno
(Baked Chicken and Potatoes)

1/4 cup olive oil
1/2 teaspoon salt
 10 pieces of chicken
 10 potatoes
1/2 teaspoon salt
1/2 teaspoon garlic powder
 1 tablespoon rosemary

Grease the bottom of a baking pan to prevent sticking. Salt the bottom of the chicken pieces and place them in the pan. Next clean the potatoes and slice them as you like. Place the potatoes in the pan around the chicken. Season the potatoes and chicken with the salt, garlic powder and rosemary. Drizzle the remaining olive oil over the potatoes and chicken. Cover the pan with foil and bake at 450 degrees for one hour. After one hour remove the foil and continue baking for an additional 45 minutes or until the chicken and potatoes are golden in color. Serves 4.

*For this dish you can use any pieces of the chicken and any type of potato.

Polpette di Carne
(Meatballs)

 1 pound ground pork
1/2 pound ground veal or beef
1/2 teaspoon salt
1/2 teaspoon black pepper
 1 teaspoon garlic powder
 2 tablespoons parmigiano cheese
 2 teaspoons parsley
 1 cup breadcrumbs
 6 eggs
 1 cup olive oil

In a large bowl, mix the pork, veal, salt, black pepper, garlic powder, parmigiano cheese, parsley and eggs. Next, add the breadcrumbs and mix well. In a frying pan cover the bottom with olive oil and heat on medium. Form the meatballs and place them in the frying pan, one next to the other with very little room between them. Turn the meatballs when they are golden on the bottom and cook the opposite side just the same. (Remove them from the pan and add them to your sauce or soup).

L'appetito viene mangiando

Cantalupo Del Sannio

Cantalupo whose name means "the singing wolf" was established around 1000 AD. Like many towns in Molise you will find trattorias and pizzerias that bring out this regions classic country dishes. This town is the home to one of the best scamorza cheese makers in the area. Their fresh ricotta and mozzarella cheeses are deliciously unforgettable.

Scamorza di Molise

PRODOTTO CON LATTE VACCINO PASTORIZZATO
CON AGGIUNTA DI FERMENTI LATTICI, CAGLIO E SALE

CASEIFICIO ARTIGIANALE PERRELLA FRANCESCO
VIA TAVERNA, 36 · TEL.0865-814314 · CANTALUPO (ISERNIA)

Dalla genuinita'

del latte locale

il Fior di Latte

DA CONSERVARSI IN FRIGO A +4° C
DA VENDERE A PESO · DA CONSUMARSI ENTRO IL:

I Dolci

Zabaglione con Frutta
(Zabaglione with Fruit)

6   egg yolks
6   tablespoons sugar
1/2   cup marsala
1   egg white
2 1/2 pounds berries of your choice

In a double boiler, add the egg yolks and sugar and beat until they become creamy. Lower the heat and add the marsala, continue beating until the mixture thickens. Take it off the heat and put the top pan into an ice water bath to stop the cooking process. Set aside to cool. Beat the egg white until stiff then fold it into the egg yolk mixture. In separate little bowls or glasses make layers of berries then zabaglione and repeat. Top with a few berries and serve. Serves 4.

Zeppolle
(Fried Dough)

4   cups water
1   tablespoon sugar
1   tablespoon yeast
7   cups flour
1   teaspoon salt
1   quart vegetable oil
     sugar to sprinkle

In a large bowl, heat the water to luke warm then add the sugar and the yeast, do not stir. Allow the yeast to sit and let it bubble for approximately 10 minutes. Gradually add the flour and salt to the yeast mixture and mix either by mixer or by hand. Continue to add the flour until the mixture is fluffy and can be spooned out like cake mix, try to avoid it being watery. Allow the mixture to rise, approximately 1-1/2 hours. In a deep skillet heat the vegetable oil. Test it to see if the oil is ready by putting in a drop of batter, when the batter rises to the top the oil is ready. Drop several tablespoons of the batter in the oil and cook until it is light golden brown. Remove and place in a large bowl and sprinkle with sugar. Continue until all the batter is gone. Serves 15-20.

Torta di Limone
(Lemon Cake)

2   cups flour
1 1/2 cups sugar
3   teaspoons baking powder
1   teaspoon salt
1/2 cup vegetable oil
7   eggs (separated)
3/4 cup cold water
2   teaspoons lemon peel (grated)
2   teaspoons vanilla
1/2 teaspoon cream of tartar

In a bowl, mix the flour, sugar, baking powder and salt. Form a well in the center and add the oil, egg yolks, water, lemon peel and vanilla. Beat with a wooden spoon until smooth. In a separate bowl beat the egg whites and cream of tartar until stiff peaks form. Pour the flour mixture into the egg white mixture and blend well. Pour into an ungreased tube pan and bake for 1 hour at 350 degrees. Serves 8.

Pandoro
(Sponge Bread)

1/4 pound butter
1/4 pound shortening
10 eggs (room temperature)
1   cup sugar
1/2 cup oil
    pinch of salt
1   tablespoon anise oil
2   lemon peels (grated)
1   cup warm water
1   tablespoon sugar
2   tablespoons yeast
10 cups flour
1/4 cup milk

In two small bowls, melt the butter in one and the shortening in the other, and set aside. In a large bowl, whisk the eggs, sugar, oil, salt, anise oil and lemon peel together. In a glass with warm water add 1 tablespoon of sugar and the yeast. Let it rise until it forms a mushroom. With a whisk, mix the melted butter and shortening into the egg mixture, then add the yeast. Add flour 1 cup at a time as you whisk until the mixture becomes stiff. Use a strong wooden spoon to keep working in the flour until it becomes difficult, then stop adding the flour but continue working it until the dough leaves the sides of the bowl. Set the bowl aside and cover it with wax paper and a dish towel and let it rise. Once the dough has risen split it in half. On your work surface take one of the halves and form a ball without compacting the dough, flatten the dough to the size of your bunt pan and make a hole in the center with your finger, stretch it open so that it will pass over the center of the pan without touching the sides and place it in a greased and flour dusted bunt pan, repeat with the other half. Cover the pans with a dish towel and let the dough rise up to the top of the pan. Once the dough has risen brush milk on the top, very lightly. Bake for 1 hour at 300 degrees. Serves 8.

Biscotti a Figura di Pesca
(Peach Cookies)

Cookie
- 4 large eggs
- 16 ounces sugar
- 12 ounces vegetable oil
- 8 ounces milk
- 48 ounces all-purpose flour
- 1 1/2 ounce baking powder

Filling
- 6 ounces espresso coffee
- 2 tablespoons almond extract
  crumbs from cookies
- 4 tablespoons cherry jam

Cookie
Mix all the ingredients together with a mixer. Form the dough into 1" balls (a little smaller then a golf ball). Place them on a baking sheet flattening one side and bake for 20 minutes at 350 degrees, until golden brown. Let them cool then carve out the center and set aside. Save the crumbs from the center in a bowl.

Filling
Mix all ingredients together to form a paste. Fill cookies with filling and put two together to form a peach.

Coloring
1/2 cup cherry whiskey with 1 drop red food coloring
1/2 cup water with 2 drops green food coloring

Dip one side of the cookie into the green water and the other side into the cherry whiskey. While the cookie is wet roll it in sugar.

Use almond strips for the stems on the cookies. Makes 3 dozen.

Tiramisu
(Pick Me Up)

- 3 egg yolks
- 3 tablespoons sugar
- 1 1/2 cups marsala liquore
- 8 ounces mascarpone cheese
- 1 cup espresso coffee
- 4 ounces whipping cream
- 1 egg white
- 24 ladyfingers

On a double boiler, add the egg yolks and sugar and beat until they become creamy. Lower the heat to a simmer. Add 1/2 cup of the marsala and continue beating until the mixture thickens. Set aside to cool.

In a bowl, mix the mascarpone cheese and 1/4 cup of espresso coffee and set aside. Whip the whipping cream until peaks form and set aside. Beat the egg white until stiff, then fold it into the egg yolk and marsala mixture. In a bowl combine the Marsala (1 cup) and espresso (3/4 cup) together and dip the ladyfingers in it so they are well absorbed. In the bowl or pan, make a layer of the dipped ladyfingers then cover with 1/2 of the mascarpone cheese mixture, then 1/2 of the egg yolk and marsala mixture and 1/2 of the cream. Repeat the layers again. Refrigerate for several hours. To create a Tiramisu that will just melt in your mouth, refrigerate for 24 hours. Serves 8.

Pan di Spagna
(Italian Sponge Cake)

Cake
- 6 eggs
- 1 1/2 cups flour
- 1 1/2 cups sugar
- 1 teaspoon baking powder
- 1/3 cup water
- 1/4 teaspoon vanilla extract
- 1/2 teaspoon lemon extract

Filling
- 1/4 cup vermouth
- 1/4 cup maraschino cherry juice
- 2 cups pastry cream

(see Crema Pasticciera recipe)

Separate the eggs. Beat the egg whites until thickened. In a bowl, sift the flour, sugar and baking powder. In another bowl, beat the egg yolks, water, vanilla and lemon extract. Add the flour mixture to the egg yolk mixture and beat until fluffy. Fold in the egg whites. Grease and flour a cake pan and pour in the batter. Bake for 1 hour and 15 minutes at 325 degrees. Serves 8.

Filling
To complete this cake, slice it in half horizontally and separate. Drizzle the vermouth and maraschino cherry juice on both sides. Next, pour half of the pastry cream on the bottom half and spread. Flip the top back on and spread the remaining cream on the top.

Crema Pasticciera
(Pastry Cream)

- 6 egg yolks
- 1 cup sugar
- 6 tablespoons flour
- 3 cups milk
- 1/4 teaspoon vanilla
- 1/2 lemon
- 2 cups fresh berries

In a large mixing bowl, blend together the egg yolks and sugar with a mixer, until fluffy. Add flour one tablespoon at a time and mix until all the lumps are gone. (If it becomes too thick while adding the flour add a little milk.) Add the milk a little at a time until all the milk is used, add the vanilla and continue mixing until well blended. Pour the mixture into a medium sauce pan and cook over medium heat. Put a fork in the end of half a lemon and use it to stir the cream to prevent sticking. (If you do not have a lemon add 1/4 teaspoon of lemon extract and stir with a wooden spoon.) Stir constantly until the cream thickens, scraping the bottom of the pan so the cream does not stick. Remove from heat and let the cream cool. Refrigerate until chilled. Serve with fresh berries. Serves 6.

Pan di Noce
(Walnut Bread)

Crust
1/4 cup warm water
1/2 cup sour cream
  1 package dry yeast
  2 tablespoons sugar
  4 cups flour
     pinch of salt
  1 cup vegetable oil
  4 egg yolks

Glaze
1/2 cup warm milk
  1 egg yolk

Filling
  1 pound ground walnuts
1/2 cup sugar
1/2 cup brown sugar
  3 eggs
1/4 teaspoon vanilla

Crust
In the warm water, add the yeast and let it sit until it forms a mushroom. Mix the sugar, flour, salt and oil in a bowl. Beat the egg yolks and add it to the mixture. Next add the sour cream and the yeast and mix well. Put the mixture on a floured bread board and knead it for about 5 minutes. Form a ball with the dough and wrap it with plastic and refrigerate for 2 hours.

Filling
Beat the eggs and add all the ingredients for the filling together and set aside. Divide the dough into 4 pieces and roll them out to 1/4" thick. Spread some filling on each piece of dough. Roll the dough to form a log. Pinch the ends together and let them rise for about 1 hour. Brush with an egg yolk and milk glaze. Bake for 40 minutes at 350 degrees. Serves 10.

Torta di Mela
(Apple Cake)

1 3/4 cups sugar
  1 cup vegetable oil
  3 eggs
  1 teaspoon salt
  1 teaspoon vanilla
  2 cups flour
  1 teaspoon baking soda
3/4 cup walnuts (chopped)
  5 large apples (chopped)

In a large bowl, add the sugar, oil, eggs, salt and vanilla and mix well. Mix the flour and baking soda together, then stir it into the egg mixture a little at a time. Add the nuts and apples and stir. Once the mixture is well blended, pour it into a greased cake pan. Bake for 55 minutes at 350 degrees. Serves 8.

Bisogna rompere la noce,
se si vuol mangiare il nocciuolo

69

Profiteroles con Crema
(Cream Puffs)

Pastry
  1 cup water
  1 teaspoon sugar
1/2 cup butter
1/4 teaspoon salt
  1 cup flour (sifted)
  4 eggs
     powdered sugar

Cream
  6 egg yolks
  1 cup sugar
  6 tablespoons flour
  3 cups milk
1/4 teaspoon vanilla
1/2 lemon

Pastry
In a medium sauce pan, mix the water, sugar, butter and salt. Heat to a boil and reduce the heat to low. Add the flour all at once and stir vigorously until the mixture leaves the sides of the pan and forms a ball. Remove from heat. Beat eggs in one at a time, beating each egg until mixture is smooth and shiny. Cool for about 15 minutes. On a greased baking sheet spoon the mixture into 24 cream puffs. Bake for 20-30 minutes at 400 degrees until they look dry and golden. Prick the puffs around the edge with the point of a knife to let the steam escape. Cool on a wire rack. When cooled, cut the puffs in half and add the chilled cream. Sprinkle the top with powder sugar. Makes 2 dozen.

Cream
In a large mixing bowl, blend together the egg yolks and sugar with a mixture until fluffy. Add flour one tablespoon at a time and mix until all the lumps are gone. (If it becomes too thick while adding the flour, add a little milk.) Add the milk a little at a time until all the milk is used, add the vanilla and continue mixing until well blended. Pour the mixture into a medium sauce pan and cook over medium heat. Put a fork in the end of half a lemon and use it to stir the cream to prevent sticking. Stir constantly until the cream thickens, scraping the bottom of the pan so the cream does not stick. Remove from heat and let the cream cool. Refrigerate until chilled.

Biscotti di Mandorle
(Almond Biscotti)

2 1/4 cups flour (sifted)
1 cup sugar
1 teaspoon baking powder
  pinch of salt
3 eggs
1 tablespoon oil
1 cup almonds (chopped)
3 tablespoons orange zest

In a large bowl, mix the flour, sugar, baking powder and salt. Make a well in the center of the flour mixture, add the eggs and oil to the center and beat with a fork, adding the flour a little at a time. Add the almonds and orange zest and work the mixture with your hands until it forms a dough. Continue kneading the dough until it becomes smooth. Divide the dough in half and form two logs, flat on the bottom making them 1 inch high. Grease and flour a baking sheet and place the logs on it. Bake for 25 minutes at 400 degrees. Remove the logs and cut them into individual cookies. Immediately place the cookies back onto the pan, cut side down, and bake for 10 additional minutes, until golden brown. Makes 2 dozen.

Santa Maria Del Molise
and
Sant'Angelo in Grotte

A vision of Saint Michael appeared in a cave where the church of Sant'Angelo in Grotte is currently located. During World War II both bells from its bell tower were taken by the Germans to make artillery. Only one bell was returned at the end of the war. The other was never returned and was replaced with a new one. This quiant little hilltop town sits above its sister town Santa Maria del Molise which has a fresh water stream that runs all year long. Many women still use this fresh water stream to do their laundry daily. It is like stepping back in time.

Roccamandolfi

On a hillside just above Cantalupo del Sannio is Roccamandolfi. This picturesque town with its white stuccoed buildings and terra cotta rooftops seem to grip onto the steep hillside. With narrow stone streets made mostly for walking it forces people to interact as they pass. "Buon'giorno!". Only occasionally do you see a little Fiat making its way up and down the narrow streets.

Other interesting towns in Molise
(Isernia, Frosolone, Campombasso, Venafro, Sessano,
S. Egidio, Guglionesi, Monti del Matese)

Printed in the United States
By Bookmasters